The Essential Over

This is a quick guide about preventing your organisation being used by money launderers

Money laundering is any means by which cash from illegal origins is made to appear legal.

Illicit cash ('dirty' money) includes the proceeds of organised crime and drug dealing, funds looted by corrupt dictators, and the money of those seeking to evade tax.

The purpose of money laundering is to clean up dirty money by disguising its origins. Launderers often try to do this by routing it through several different bank accounts before turning it into an investment in a legitimate financial instrument or business.

Financial institutions and advisers – banks, investment banks, stockbrokers, accountants, solicitors, and insurers – need to be fully aware of their legal obligations to combat money laundering.

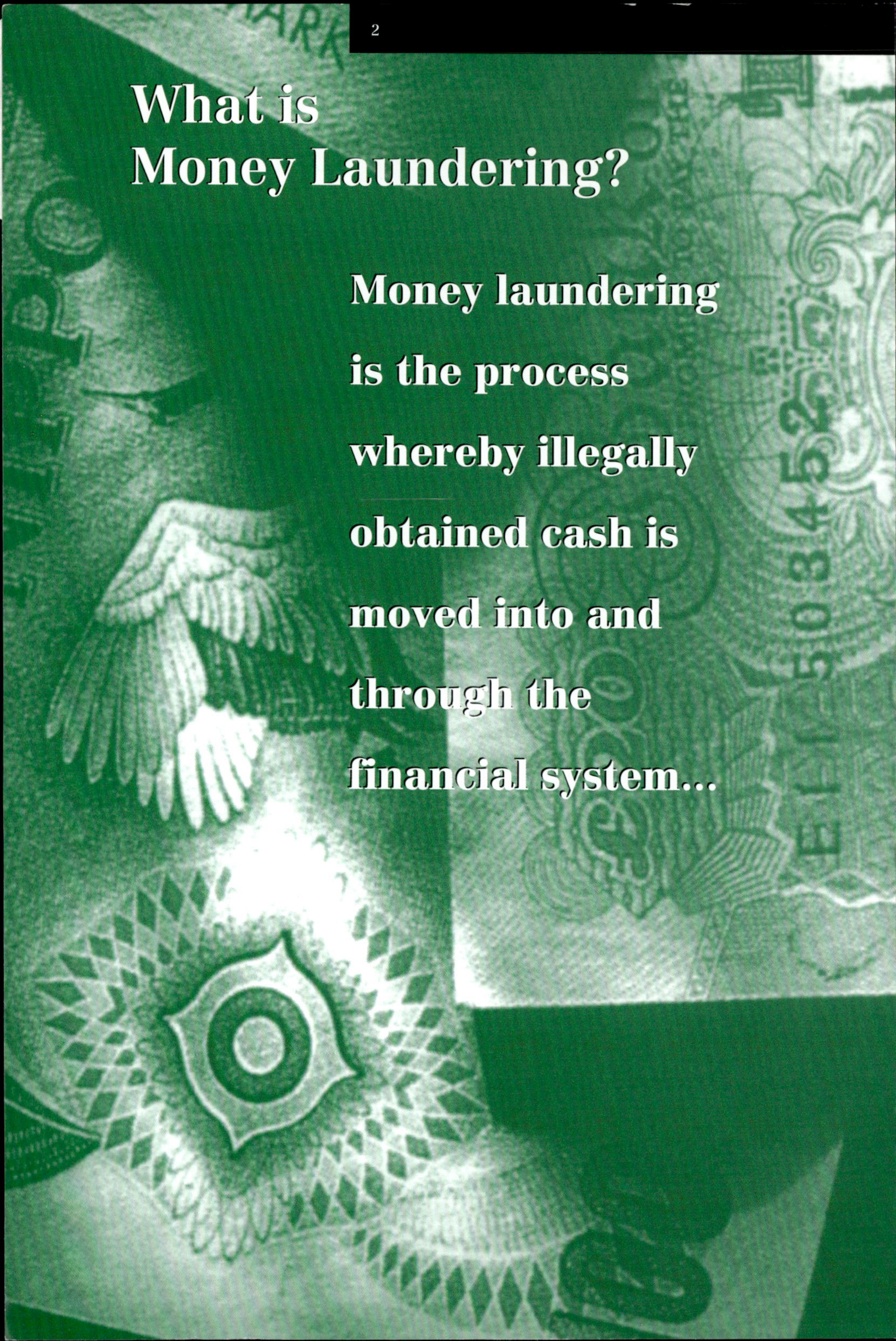

What is Money Laundering?

Money laundering is the process whereby illegally obtained cash is moved into and through the financial system...

Key issues

- By law any financial organisation which suspects it has dealt directly or indirectly with a money launderer must report its suspicions to the authorities.
- Financial organisations are in the front line in the battle with money launderers. This is because in laundering dirty cash, criminals need to use the banking and securities systems.
- Identifying suspicious transactions can be difficult. Intermediaries, such as correspondent banks, can be unwitting conduits for laundered funds.
- The sheer volume of potentially suspicious transactions requires considerable vigilance. The advent of internet banking, electronic purses and encryption has added to the problem.
- There have been several high profile cases involving major money centre banks. These show that even the biggest banks are vulnerable to the attentions of launderers.
- At the other end of the scale, smaller scale launderers also use casinos, bookmakers, auction houses, and bureaux de change.

- The UK regulations governing attempts to control money laundering are part of the *Criminal Justice Act 1993*. The *Financial Services and Markets Act 2000* updated the UK's legal framework in this area. The US has strict laws governing payments to and from suspect individuals and organisations.

- Every organisation involved in the financial community (banks, securities houses, accountants and solicitors) must appoint a *Money Laundering Reporting Officer* (MLRO). The role of the MLRO is to gather and channel reports of suspicious transactions to the authorities.

- Technology has made it easier for criminals to move money around. But it can also aid control and detection of suspicious transactions.

- Combating money laundering is vital in the fight against crime and to preserve the integrity of the financial system.

Why controlling money laundering is important

What is money laundering?

Money laundering is the way that cash generated from illegal activities, especially drug dealing and other forms of organised crime, moves clandestinely into the legitimate economy.

Money laundering experts identify three phases in the laundering process:

- *Placement* – this is where paper money from criminal activity is converted into a negotiable instrument. This is so that it can be infiltrated into the banking system.
- *Layering* – once placed in this way, the funds are inserted into the banking system either in small amounts or, if in big amounts, moved around quickly. In both instances, the objective is to disguise their origin.
- *Integration* – the laundered funds are brought back into circulation as some form of legitimate business or investment.

The *placement* stage is the point at which the launderers are at their most vulnerable. Favourite means by which funds are laundered include using cash to purchase any of the following:

- airline tickets
- travellers cheques
- cars and car leases
- art and antiques
- designer luggage
- thoroughbred racehorses
- gaming chips
- single premium insurance bonds
- traded endowment policies
- futures and options.

All of these have been used for money laundering. The launderer later sells the ‘instruments’ in return for payment by cheque or electronic funds transfer. This enables their covert transfer into the banking system.

The introduction of Euro notes and coins on January 1st 2002 has significance for money laundering. The scenario is one of launderers taking advantage of the high volume of 'old' notes and coins being exchanged during the changeover period to place illicit 'old' money into the system and receive 'clean' Euro notes in return.

A particular issue vis–à–vis placement relates to high denomination banknotes. High denomination banknotes mean that large quantities of cash become more easily portable. Though the €500 note is roughly equivalent to the DM1000 banknote, in many EU countries it is many times larger than the previous highest denomination note.

German politicians have been keen to see the advent of high denomination Euro banknotes. This is in order to persuade their populations that the change to the Euro is a seamless one.

The scale of the problem

Money laundering is a big problem. It has grown in tandem with the drugs trade, and with the greater mobility of capital that has come in the wake of the globalisation of financial markets.

The extent of money laundering can be gauged by the following:

- Cash generated by the trade in illicit drugs is estimated at more than $5000bn worldwide per annum. A substantial proportion of this is laundered. The *International Monetary Fund* (IMF) believes that anything from $500bn to $1500bn is laundered each year. In a good year $750m of laundered cash is recovered – a minute fraction of the total.

- The banking system handles more than a million electronic transfers of funds every day. This means that detecting funds once they have entered the system is difficult. The scale of funds transfers can be gauged by the fact that Euro payments systems alone are believed to handle some €700bn daily. The largest bank in America handles $1trillion a day in wire transfers.

- Launderers can exploit offshore financial centres if controls are lax. Offshore banks operating in tax havens control some $5000bn in assets.

- The scale of the funds being laundered suggests that virtually every bank or financial institution will be regularly approached by, or have unwittingly dealt with, a money launderer.

- Constant vigilance is required. One reason for this is that the resources that the launderers have their disposals are much bigger than the budgets normally made available by governments to fight crime of this sort.

Why combating it is important

Banks and other financial institutions are particularly vulnerable to money laundering. Recent cases have shown that inadequate attempts to police money laundering can generate very adverse publicity.

There are a number of reasons why institutions must be aware of their obligations in this area:

- Knowingly assisting money laundering is against the law. There are severe penalties for those found guilty, not to mention the adverse publicity convictions attract.

- Failing to detect money laundering is highly embarrassing. It also generates a huge volume of negative publicity. This is particularly so if the institution concerned is a large and prominent one.

- Self-interest alone makes it vital for firms and their employees to be aware of the law in this respect and to follow it to the letter.

- Successful money laundering means that organised crime has cash available to fund further illicit activities.

- Making it more difficult for criminals to launder their ill-gotten gains is an effective weapon in the fight against crime.

- Successful money laundering damages the integrity of the financial system, and public confidence in it.

Money laundering and the law

The UK's legal framework

In the UK, several Acts of Parliament and statutory controls govern the attempts to stamp out money laundering. Professionals in banking and securities have a duty to be fully aware of their provisions.

Attempts to control money laundering through the legal system are comparatively recent.

Money laundering was first categorised as a criminal offence in the UK in the *Drug Trafficking Offences Act 1986*. Subsequently this law was extended to cover laundering the proceeds of all crime and various other provisions were added. The legal framework was further refined in 1994.

The *Criminal Justice Act 1993* consolidated and extended the earlier legal framework governing money laundering. Included within it were some of the provisions of an earlier European Commission directive. Specific regulations, based on the Act, were issued covering money laundering.

The effect of these changes was to place the onus on the financial institutions to introduce appropriate internal procedures. These are aimed at detecting and avoiding their firms being the unwitting vehicle for money laundering. The procedures include customer identification, staff training, systems development and other measures.

The 1993 Act makes it an offence to assist a money launderer in concealing, retaining or investing funds if that person knows or suspects that the cash came from serious criminal conduct.

Punishment on conviction is severe.

- Those who knowingly assist money launderers face up to fourteen years in prison, a heavy fine, *or both*;
- Failing to report knowledge or a suspicion of money laundering is punishable by a fine, up to five years in prison, *or both*;
- Tipping–off money launderers that suspicions have been disclosed to the authorities also carry the same penalties.
- Failing to observe the regulations is punishable by a fine or up to two years in prison *or both* – irrespective of whether or not any money laundering has taken place.

The *Financial Services and Markets Act 2000* further defines the role of money laundering regulations for London–based financial institutions. The Act gives the Financial Services Authority *four statutory objectives*, one of which is to reduce financial crime. In the Act, financial crime encompasses criminal market misconduct, fraud, and money laundering.

Under the Act the FSA has the power to make and enforce rules with respect to money laundering. These will set standards for anti–money laundering systems and controls in FSA–regulated businesses.

The essence of the rules will be to encourage businesses:

- to take care when dealing with new customers, to be alert to the possibility of money laundering by a customer or prospective customer;
- to communicate suspicions to the criminal authorities;
- to keep records of sufficient quality to be used in subsequent prosecutions;
- to ensure senior management oversight;
- to secure and maintain the informed participation in these systems of all relevant employees within the business.

There are other issues the FSA wishes to see addressed. One is that investment banks take particular care when dealing with the treasury operations of private companies. Another is where business is introduced by a third party, that they satisfy themselves that the introducer has conducted rigorous checks on the provenance of customer funds.

The Money Laundering Reporting Officer (MLRO)

The 1993 Act and the associated Money Laundering Regulations require every firm in the financial sector to appoint a Money Laundering Reporting Officer (MLRO). The *Financial Services and Markets Act 2000* clarified the details of the MLRO's duties. You should know who your MLRO is, and what he or she does.

Money Laundering Reporting Officers are vital to ensure that firms comply with the laws and regulations described above.

Who this individual is will depend on the nature and size of the firm. However, the regulations require that the MLRO is sufficiently senior to command authority within the firm. Within small firms it may be the senior partner or chief executive, or the finance director or administration partner. Within larger firms it is likely to be a senior member of the compliance or internal audit team.

The MLRO is responsible for:

- *Ensuring* that staff are trained on a regular basis to identify potentially suspicious transactions.
- *Verifying*, according to pre–set guidelines, whether or not potentially suspicious transactions are, in fact, suspicious and should be reported.

- *Reporting* suspicious transactions and liaising with the authorities over any further action to be taken.

The MLRO is expected to act honestly and reasonably and to make determinations in good faith. Provided that this is done, the MLRO will not be held liable for failing to report a transaction which later turns out to be suspicious.

The law requires staff to report potentially suspicious transactions to their MLRO or a designated deputy. They must provide reasonable access to any further information the MLRO may require, to gauge whether or not a transaction should be reported.

They must also cooperate in any subsequent related investigations. Written records must be kept of every potentially suspicious transaction and strict confidentiality is essential. The legislation also protects those who report suspicions of money laundering from being sued for breaking client confidentiality.

New measures

There are several new developments to be aware of.

In particular these include:

- extending the scope of the reporting requirements to include company formation agents and providers of corporate services;
- requiring bureaux de change to register details of their ownership. In countries where this has been introduced, more than half of the bureaux have closed rather than register;
- having the power to be able to freeze funds without having proved a crime has taken place;
- lowering the burden of proof in instances where criminal cash can be confiscated;
- removing barriers to the exchange of confidential information between the police, financial regulators and the Inland Revenue.

International Action on Money Laundering

Because banking and securities markets are increasingly global, international co-ordination of, and cooperation on action against money laundering is essential.

Research has shown that 80% of money laundering transactions have an international component. There are several forums for international action on money laundering.

Financial Action Task Force (FATF)

The Financial Action Task Force is an offshoot of the *Organisation for Economic Cooperation and Development* (OECD).

Set up in 1989, the FATF currently has some 31 members. It is charged with coordinating international anti–money laundering measures.

The FATF has issued some 40 recommendations, applicable internationally, on how member countries can best combat money laundering.

Any financial institutions based in a FATF–member country can be assumed to have passed a so–called *equivalence test*. The FATF has also agreed a process whereby other countries can acquire FATF accreditation. Its efforts continue to be hampered by the fact that many countries are not members of the organisation.

MLCA and OFAC

Banks and securities firms with subsidiaries or affiliates in the USA are also subject to the anti–money laundering regulations of the USA.

Anti–money laundering legislation in the USA is enshrined in the *Money Laundering Control Act 1986*. Amendments to the *Banking Secrecy Act* in the early 1990s were also made with a view to combating money laundering. The US Treasury *Office of Foreign Assets Control* (OFAC) administers other controls on money laundering and related activity.

This organisation maintains a list of countries, organisations and individuals to which payment through the banking system should not be made. These include known companies or individuals associated with organised crime, drug–dealing and terrorism.

UK banks and securities firms need to be aware of the OFAC rules because:

- If the organisation (say, a UK investment bank) has a subsidiary in the USA it is subject to the provisions of the OFAC regulations.
- Payment to the proscribed individual or organisation does not have to be made via the US to contravene the regulations.
- Penalties are severe if a contravention is detected, and include multi–million dollar fines.

- The OFAC 'black list' is updated regularly and currently runs to 14 closely–typed pages. Monitoring the list for changes on a regular basis, or having a system for doing so, is important.

Systems have also been specifically developed, both internally by banks and by commercial software providers, to handle the issues raised by complying with the OFAC rules.

These programs sit inside existing settlement systems and monitor transactions, comparing them with the names contained on the OFAC list. Typically these programs will automatically update the OFAC black list daily by downloading the revised list from the OFAC web pages.

There have been periodic signs that the US is also moving to enforce anti–money laundering legislation on any foreign institution if a suspect transaction passes, however briefly, through the US banking system.

Other International Action

The EU has an anti–money laundering Directive; several member states have taken their own initiatives on money laundering and in many cases these go beyond the minimum levels of implementation of the current directive.

In July 2000 the FATF published a list of 15 jurisdictions where it said that serious systematic problems had been identified. These included a number of Caribbean and South Pacific tax havens as well as countries like Israel, Russia, Liechtenstein, and Panama. Liechtenstein, the Cayman Islands, the Bahamas and Panama have since been removed from the list. Egypt, Guatemala, Hungary, Indonesia, Nigeria and Burma were added to it in July 2001.

Banking anonymity remains an issue in some areas, although it is gradually being eradicated.

Liechtenstein recently agreed to insist that trustees and lawyers opening accounts on behalf of clients must in future name the beneficiaries of those accounts. Existing accounts have been given two years to comply with the new rules.

Austria has also scrapped its system of anonymous savings bank passbooks, partly because of pressure from the European Union and to avoid being suspended from the FATF.

In October 2000, eleven of the world's biggest banks signed an agreement on guidelines covering due diligence actions to be taken to avoid money laundering in private banking. These are called the *Wolfsburg principles*.

The principles are heavily based on a 'know your customer' approach, establishing first and foremost that a client's wealth can reasonably be supposed to have derived from a legitimate activity. They go on to identify situations that might require additional attention, how to report suspicious transactions, and staff education.

Detection & Enforcement

Detection and enforcement

Recognising and reporting suspicious transactions is a vital part of combating money laundering, although some sections of the financial community appear to report a very small number of transactions. There are several indicators that betray suspicious activity.

NCIS

In the UK, reports of suspicious transactions related to money laundering are handled by the *Economic Crime Unit* of the *National Criminal Intelligence Service* (NCIS).

Reports can be filed either in paper form or electronically but must be in a standard format and disclose sufficient information to allow NCIS to make a judgement about the nature of the suspicion and to obtain a court order if necessary. NCIS may then seek further information from the institution involved.

A written receipt of a report will normally be given and in most cases the transaction will be allowed to continue (so as not to arouse suspicion). In exceptional circumstances (for example, an imminent arrest) permission to continue with a transaction may be withheld.

Firms should ensure that their own staff are warned about the suspicious transaction, that legal advice is taken and that any other necessary steps are taken to protect the firm.

The *Economic Crime Unit* of NCIS is staffed by police and Customs officers. Reports of suspicious transactions remain confidential to NCIS and are not passed to any other arm of government. Maintaining confidential relationships with the financial community is considered by them to be very important.

NCIS received over 18,000 reports of suspicious transactions in 2000. To put it in perspective, this compares with around 2,000 in 1990 and 15,000 in 1994, just after the regulations came into force and awareness was at it height.

Banks make up the vast bulk of suspicious transaction reports. Accountants and solicitors appear to report suspicious transactions infrequently. Rules on client confidentiality may dissuade some members of these latter professions from reporting their suspicions, even though the law protects them in this respect.

Recognising suspicious transactions

Defining a suspicious transaction is very difficult, especially in the securities industry. Most will appear to originate from bona fide sources and will not be as obvious as an individual turning up with a briefcase full of money.

A suspicious transaction should, however, be easier to detect if the institution is aware of, or can monitor, the normal pattern of behaviour of each of its customers. Anything out of the ordinary can then be investigated further. New clients need particular scrutiny. Several general questions should be asked in respect of each transaction:

- Do you know the customer personally?
- Is the transaction in keeping with what he, she or it normally does?
- Is the customer dealing more frequently and in larger size than normal?
- Is the role of an agent in the transaction usual?
- Are there any linked transactions which appear suspicious?

Who's responsible?

The responsibility for identifying and reporting suspicious transactions inevitably falls most heavily on staff involved in dealing directly with customers and processing transactions.

Dealers, *sales people* and *settlement staff* all need to be aware of their obligations in helping to combat money laundering.

Front office staff need to be aware of their legal responsibilities in this area and in particular of the organisation's policy for dealing with new or occasional customers, especially where large sums of cash or bearer securities are involved.

Back office staff also need to be aware of their legal responsibilities in this area and in particular to watch for abnormal settlement or delivery instructions. Other elementary procedures need to be observed – for instance, matching of the identity of an investor with the cheque received in settlement of a transaction.

Some Pointers

There are common characteristics in many transactions that involve money laundering.

Money laundering may be a possibility in the following cases:

New clients...

- where verification of their identity is unusually difficult;
- where, in the case of a corporate client, delays accompany a request for documents;
- with no discernible need for using your firm's services;
- with a distant address who could find the same service nearer home;
- introduced by entities in areas where drug production or trafficking is common;

- habitually dealing with a counterparty you do not know;
- who wish to use an intermediary but have no apparent need to do so.

Dealing patterns which involve...

- large numbers of deals across various jurisdictions;
- buying and selling for no apparent reason – ie 'churning' at the client's request;
- unusual deal size, careless instructions or excessive activity;
- low–quality securities bought overseas and switched into high–grade ones in the UK;
- bearer stock held outside a recognised custodial system;
- frequent small purchases for cash, which are then aggregated and sold;
- early termination at a loss of packaged investment products bought with cash;
- refunds related to the above where payment is requested to be made to a third party.

Settlement and delivery which involves...

- the use of large amounts of cash;
- settlement of large deals by third parties;
- the use of bearer securities from outside a recognised custodial system;
- payment to an apparently unconnected third party;
- registration or delivery of stock to an apparently unconnected third party.

These lists are by no means exhaustive, but the reasons for regarding transactions like this as suspicious are obvious. They do not necessarily indicate that money laundering is taking place, merely that further investigation of the client should take place.

Recent cases and new developments

The following are brief details of some recent cases where money laundering appears to have occurred. They are highlighted to demonstrate some of the methods used and how the perpetrators were able to escape detection for some time.

Mexican Banks

According to press reports, the Mexican banking system has proved particularly susceptible to the depredations of launderers. In 1995 members of the Juarez drug cartel bought control of a small domestic bank, *Grupo Financiero Anahuac*, and laundered tens of millions of dollars through it before the ruse was discovered by a regulatory audit a year or so later.

In 1999 *Banca Serfin* and *Bancomer* pleaded guilty to money laundering charges following an undercover ‘sting’ operation conducted by US agencies. The significance of the case was that the judge concerned did not allow the companies to dissociate themselves from the actions of the employees concerned.

In return for pleading guilty and accepting confiscation of the cash involved, the banks were allowed to retain their banking licenses.

US Banks

In February 2000, a former employee of a major US bank and her husband admitted in court that they had laundered at least $7bn through the bank over three years, much of it from Russian nationals.

A UK private company controlled by the employee's husband was the main conduit for the operation. Another bank employee was also involved in the scheme.

The bank was ignorant of the scheme and cooperated fully with the authorities in the subsequent investigation, although it did admit that suspicions raised by other employees' about the accounts had not been followed up sufficiently vigorously.

Regulators later imposed a strict system of audits and beefed up training and compliance on the bank, many of which had already been implemented by the time the order had been made.

In the wake of the case, another major US bank also admitted that internal investigations had uncovered evidence that more than $725m in questionable Russian funds has passed through its accounts over a nine-year period from 1991 onwards.

US Banks and Caribbean 'shells'

In early 2001 minority staff members working for the *US Senate Permanent Subcommittee on Investigations* published a report that claimed that major US banks had unwittingly handled substantial quantities of laundered cash because of insufficiently close monitoring of correspondent banking relationships.

The report focused particularly on accounts held in *shell banks* (banks with no physical presence) in jurisdictions with tight banking secrecy laws.

The US banks were mentioned in the report as having weak due diligence and inadequate anti-laundering controls. The banks acknowledged that the breaches had occurred but stressed, in a letter to legislators, that the sums involved were less than one tenth of one per cent of their total payments in the period in question. The banks are developing a joint code of practice on the issue.

General Abacha

In March 2001 the *Financial Services Authority* (FSA) reported that 23 banks in London had handled $1.3bn of transactions on behalf of the family and friends of the late dictator of Nigeria, General Sani Abacha. The funds represent a significant part of the estimated $2-4bn looted from Nigeria during the general's five-year rule.

The banks were not named by the FSA, but the investigation was prompted by requests from the present Nigerian government for accounts to be frozen and documents seized at fifteen London banks.

The FSA report found that fifteen of the twenty three banks investigated had significant control weakness. Eight of the banks were said to have corrected the weaknesses since they had been drawn to their attention.

Weaknesses identified at the banks included inadequate senior management oversight of account opening by higher-risk customers, weaknesses in verifying the beneficial owners of companies, over-reliance on introductions from existing customers, inadequate understanding of the sources of a customer's wealth, failure to report suspicions with sufficient rigour, and weaknesses in record keeping and retrieval.

The banks concerned were set strict deadlines to implement remedial action.

Slobodan Milosevic

Britain's FSA has been involved in helping to track down money filched from Yugoslavia under the Milosevic regime. Most of the money is believed to have left the country through Cyprus, Greece, Israel and Switzerland, but British-based banks may also have been involved in handling money taken out of the country following privatisation of the state telecoms monopoly in 1997.

Three Greek banks are suspected of doing business with former President Milosevic and Greece has since announced that it is to tighten up its anti-money laundering measures.

Newer concerns

The advent of the Internet and world wide web, electronic banking, smart cards and other such concepts create problems for those attempting to monitor flows of illicit cash. Some of the issues include:

Web–based financial services not only provide an easy access point for criminals, but their nature means that the link between the customer and the institution is depersonalised. This is a major concern of those responsible for enforcement, as is the potential jurisdictional issue that can arise from having servers located offshore.

The latest FATF report on money laundering trends and methods identifies how fraud and laundering through electronic banks can take place.

Internet gambling is becoming a major issue. Just as land–based casinos have been used for money laundering, so cyber–casinos offer a more effective means, since servers can be located in offshore jurisdictions and all transactions are credit card and software–based, making reconstructing evidence very difficult.

Electronic cash in the form of 'electronic purses' or similar 'stored value cards' remove the need for large quantities of cash to be transported, provided a friendly issuer can be co–opted. There is pressure for such cards to have limited capacity for precisely this reason.

Some other e–money systems allow one–way privacy, permitting senders to check that money has been received by the intended recipient, but do not reveal to the recipient, or an investigator, where the money has originated from. There is pressure on those designing e–cash systems to include a compulsory electronic audit trail in their specifications.

Encryption capabilities in the hands of private individuals remain a concern for the authorities. Launderers could use these to move money from jurisdiction to jurisdiction without detection. A related development in the UK has put in place a system that will allow security and intelligence agencies to gain access to 'encryption keys' used to scramble electronic communications.

The advent of sophisticated computer–based techniques is not, however, solely to the advantage of would–be launderers.

Computer software is becoming more sophisticated and better able to detect unusual patterns in transactions. There is probably no substitute for the human factor in recognising whether a transaction 'smells right' or not. Nonetheless computer systems have been developed to assist in the identification of suspicious transactions.

Some systems banks and securities firms are building internal systems to do this. Others are being developed on their behalf by consultants and software firms. Systems used to detect fraud by employees can also be adapted to handle money laundering issues.

Many of the systems being developed use artificial intelligence techniques. They take the recent patterns of transactions by individual clients over a particular period of time and 'learn' from them to spot unusual deals.

Glossary

Artificial Intelligence

Computer technique simulating human thought processes

Bearer Security

Security which is unregistered and therefore the property of the bearer

Custodial System

Recognised body through which securities are registered and cleared

Economic Crime Unit

Part of NCIS responsible for combating money laundering

Electronic Purses

Smart card able to store monetary credit in electronic form

E–Money

Money held by an individual in electronic form

FATF

Financial Action Task Force

FSA

Financial Services Authority

Integration

The completion of the laundering process

Layering

Insertion of ‘immersed’ funds into the banking system

MLRO

Money Laundering Reporting Officer

Money Laundering

Conversion of illicit cash into a legitimate investment

NCIS

National Criminal Intelligence Service

OFAC

Office of Foreign Assets Control (of the US Treasury)

Packaged Investment Products

Investments such as OEICs, unit trusts etc

Placement

Conversion of illicit cash into a negotiable instrument

Single Premium Insurance Bond

Investment product acquired by payment of a lump sum

Suspicious Transactions

Potential money laundering deal to be reported to MLRO

Web addresses

Bank of England:	http://www.bankofengland.co.uk
DTI:	http://www.dti.gov.uk
European Commission:	http://europa.eu.int
HM Treasury:	http://www.hm-treasury.gov.uk
FATF:	http://www.oecd.org/fatf/
NCIS:	http://www.ncis.co.uk
FSA:	http://www.fsa.gov.uk
British Bankers Association:	http://www.bba.org.uk

Useful contacts and references

Bank of England

Public Enquiries Group (HO–1)
Threadneedle Street
London EC2R 8AH
Tel: 020 7601 4878

Department of Trade and Industry

Kingsgate House
66–74 Victoria Street
London SW1E 6SW
Tel: 020 7215 5000

European Commission

Refer to local EU information offices
throughout the country.
Tel: 020 7973 1992

HM Treasury

Parliament Street
London SW1P 3AG
Public Enquiry Office
Tel: 020 7270 4558
See also their website at: http://www.hm–treasury.gov.uk

Financial Action Task Force on Money Laundering (FATF)

http://www.oecd.org/fatf

National Criminal Intelligence Service (NCIS)

PO Box 8000

London SE11 5EN

Tel: 020 7238 8000

Financial Services Authority (FSA)

25 The North Colonnade

Canary Wharf

London E14 5HS

Tel: 020 7676 1000

Fax: 020 7676 1099

British Bankers' Association

105–108 Old Broad Street

London EC2N 1EX

Tel: 020 7216 8800

Other Securities Institute titles

Each publication provides a detailed overview and practical introduction to key topics within financial services.

The two titles in our *Essential Elements* series – Economic & Monetary Union and Money Laundering – provide rapid briefing on key issues as they arise. Each booklet contains the relevant facts and figures to give you an overview of the subject.

Our *Griffin Guide* range consists of re–worked and updated notes from our popular courses. These publications are a useful reference for everyone who needs to grasp the basics of a topic – fast!

Essential Elements

Essential Elements of the Prevention of Money Laundering

This quick guide looks at the scale of the problem and efforts taken to overcome it: an essential reference for all who are concerned to identify attempts at money laundering within their organisation.

- What is money laundering?
- Money laundering and the law
- How do you spot it in the process, and what to do.

£4.99 48pp paperback, ISBN: 1 84307 005 7, 2nd edition

Essential Elements of Economic & Monetary Union

Economic and Monetary Union (EMU) is the system that links together the economies and currencies of the participating European countries. The European Central Bank has become responsible for centralised monetary policy. What does the Euro mean for you?

- Convergence
- Impact of the Euro on the markets
- Preparing for the future.

£4.99 28pp paperback, ISBN: 1 900520 31 1

Griffin Guides

The Fundamentals of CREST

The Fundamentals of CREST gives a detailed overview of securities administration and settlement through the CREST system. It is illustrated throughout with diagrams and tables, bullet points and summaries.

- Handling Certificated Securities
- Corporate Actions and Claims
- Stock Loans and Collateral.

£14.99 128pp paperback, ISBN: 1 900520 98 2
2nd edition

An Introduction to Corporate Finance – Transactions and Techniques

Introduction to Corporate Finance provides readers with the key elements of corporate finance. The book introduces the principle techniques used in corporate finance, combined with practical experience and hands–on, numerically orientated case studies.

- Sources of Capital
- Flotations/Initial Public Offerings
- Mergers and Acquisitions
- Management Buy Outs
- Determining the Cost of Capital
- International Equity Offerings
- Valuing Securities
- Well illustrated with diagrams and tables, bullet points and summaries.

£19.99 96pp paperback, ISBN: 1 900520 09 5

An Introduction to Swaps

An Introduction to Swaps gives a detailed overview of how the various categories of swap work, how they are traded and what they are used for. Topics include interest rate swaps, managing risk, asset swaps, currency swaps. The book is illustrated with over 50 diagrams and tables.

- Managing risk with swaps
- Asset swaps
- Currency swaps.

£19.99 160pp paperback, ISBN: 1 900520 21 4

An Introduction to Fund Management

An Introduction to Fund Management introduces readers to the economic rationale for the existence of funds, the different types available, investment strategies and many other related issues from the perspective of the investment manager. Topics include the features and characteristics of funds, portfolio management and administration, performance measurement and investment mathematics. Includes relevant formulae, equations and examples.

- Features and characteristics of funds
- Portfolio management and administration
- Performance measurement
- Investment mathematics.

£19.99 160pp paperback, ISBN: 1 900520 61 3

An Introduction to Value–at–Risk

An Introduction to Value–at–Risk has been written for those with little or no previous understanding of or exposure to the concepts of risk management and Value–at–Risk. Topics include applications of VaR, instrument structures, stress testing, VaR for corporates, credit risk and legal/regulatory issues.

- Risk and Risk management
- VaR and Derivatives, Fixed Interest products.
- VaR for Corporates

£19.99 208pp paperback, ISBN: 1 900520 63 X, 2nd edition

Introduction to Equity Markets

Introduction to Equity Markets provides an overview of the current financial services industry. The book introduces the reader to different types of companies and shares as well as analysis of UK markets. An overview of dealing and settlement in some of the world's major markets is also featured. Contents include:

- Shareholders and Company Law
- Issuing Shares – The Primary Market
- Trading Shares – The Secondary Market
- Settlement of Transactions
- Major Overseas Exchanges and Indices
- Dividends, Bonus Issues and Rights Issues
- Company Accounts.

£19.99 170pp paperback, ISBN: 1 900520 71 0

Introduction to Repo Markets

An Introduction to Repo Markets provides a comprehensive description and analysis of the repo markets. The text has been written to cater for those with little or no previous experience of the repo markets, though it also develops the subject matter to sufficient depth to be of use to more experienced practitioners. Contents include:

- Uses and economic functions of repo
- Accounting, Tax and Capital issues
- The UK gilt repo market
- The implied repo rate and basis trading
- Repo and the yield curve

£19.99 240pp paperback, ISBN: 1 900520 86 9 2nd edition

Introduction to Bond Markets

Introduction to Bond Markets provides a comprehensive, authoritative description and analysis of the bond markets. The book considers basic 'plain vanilla' bonds and elementary bond mathematics, before looking at the array of different instruments available. Contents include:

- Bond Yield Measurement
- Corporate Debt Markets
- Eurobonds
- Introduction to Repo
- Risk Management
- Off-Balance Sheet Instruments
- Government Bond Markets
- Emerging Bond Markets.

£19.99 410pp paperback, ISBN: 1 900520 79 6, 2nd edition

Introduction to the Gilt Strips Market

Introduction to the Gilt Strips Market provides a thorough description and analysis of gilt strips. The contents describe and define strips as a financial instrument and examine the use and application of gilt strips within the context of the capital markets as a whole. Contents include:

- Zero–coupon bonds
- The yield curve
- Interest rate risk for strips
- Settlement, tax and regulatory issues
- Trading and strategy

£19.99 192pp paperback, ISBN: 1 900520 91 5

Dictionary of Financial & Securities Terms

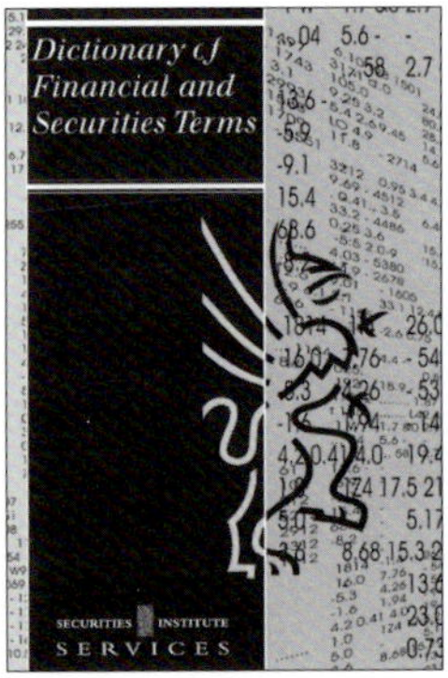

This dictionary is intended to give a quick, clear and straight forward definition of frequently used terms in the financial and securities industry. Also included is a comprehensive listing of abbreviations and acronyms.

- What is a Bill of Exchange?
- What does SPAN stand for?
- What are CHIPS and CHAPS?
- What is the standard definition of EPS?

Approximately 1,500 entries. Included with the dictionary is a FREE CD–ROM version for users to load onto their PC for easy reference at home or at work.

£17.99 240pp paperback, ISBN: 1 900520 96 6

For further details on these and other new titles, contact our Client Services Department on *020 7645 0680*
